AF248546

# BADGES OF THE BRITISH ARMY PRICE GUIDE

In recent years, there have been great changes in the hobby of badge collecting; not only has the hobby become even more popular, but a considerable amount of new research has been undertaken. While there remain gaps in the story of the badges of the British Army (for many variations and special patterns are still unexplained), available knowledge on the subject has increased enormously. This has created a greater demand for badges and, coupled to the disastrous effects of inflation, it has pushed up prices to figures thought impossible a few years ago.

In these circumstances, it was felt that new collectors might welcome some guidance on the relative prices of badges. With this object in mind this special section has been added in which every badge illustrated in the book has been priced. The figure given (to the nearest pound) is for a genuine badge in good condition – but it cannot be emphasised too strongly that this can only be a guide, for there may be several recorded variations, which could be worth more than the suggested amount. Rarity affects the price, and Victorian and Edwardian specimens will usually be worth much more than an example of a more recent date.

The difficulty in assessing a realistic price is made even greater by the fact that it takes time to publish and distribute a book. It was therefore necessary to guess what the trend of prices was likely to be, and to forecast the probable going price at the time when this book reaches the reader.

Another big change has been the impact on the market of 'restrikes' – modern copies of badges – and their manufacture has become quite a sizeable industry. Production techniques include good quality casting and stamping from original dies or modern, specially commissioned dies. Some are obvious copies that would deceive few collectors, and these can be accepted for what they are. The problem arises from the top quality pieces, which are so good that they can deceive even the most experienced of collectors. When these are offered on the market as genuine, original pieces, then confidence is undermined and the hobby suffers. It is not unknown for restrikes to be specially treated in order to age them; for such tricks there can be no defence – they are blatantly dishonest. It is easy to warn the collector against this unpleasant and dishonest trend, but much harder to offer advice on how to spot the 'dud'. One of the best approaches is to find a reputable dealer, and rely on his skill and experience. Much benefit can be obtained by joining a local militaria society, where experienced collectors will probably be prepared to help by allowing the beginner to handle and examine genuine items.

When buying a badge, always examine it carefully: original badges were cheap to produce, and imperfect specimens were never issued, so each badge should be examined for any flaws or imperfect details. Check that the badge has been properly finished – very rough or irregular edges, particularly at the back, could well indicate a restrike. Examine the lugs or sliders, particularly the method of fixing, as silver solder is widely used on modern restrikes. Repairers may also use silver solder, but they do not try to disguise the fact; restrike dealers frequently darken the solder by chemical treatment. Do not be fooled by the appearance of age – it is not at all difficult to add many years to the look of a badge. Finally, watch dealers' lists with care and, if rare badges figure frequently and repetitively, be cautious, and wonder at the source of supply!

Finally I would like to express my sincere thanks to many friends for their help in preparing this price guide, particularly to Laurie Archer, on whose expertise I drew heavily.

## NOTE TO THE 1980/81 EDITION
A continuing high demand has meant that many prices have risen since the 1978 list was published. Something like two-thirds of the badges now cost more.

The prices listed apply to genuine badges, but, unfortunately, many restrikes are now being offered as originals. Improved production techniques have made it even more difficult to detect restrikes, and the collector needs to be very careful.

The completion of an outstanding work on badges was achieved when Volume 2 of *Head-Dress Badges of the British Army* by A. L. Kipling and H. L. King was published late in 1979 (Volume 1 having appeared in 1978). This indispensable work contains a useful chapter on restrikes by Laurie Archer. It is to be hoped that this same expert will assemble and publish the notes on restrikes that he has included in many of his badge lists. All badge collectors would find them of use.                                                                                 F. W., 1980

## NOTE TO THE 1982/83 EDITION
Prices of the more common items have not changed appreciably over the last year, but the opposite is true of the scarcer items. Their value has increased considerably and this trend is almost certain to continue. Restrikes/copies continue to proliferate, and their quality and detail improve constantly.                    F. W., 1982

## NOTE TO THE 1984/85 EDITION
During the past year there has been the inevitable rise in value of almost all the badges covered by this volume. The largest rises have been, not surprisingly, for the rarer badges, as an increasing demand chases a diminishing supply. Re-strikes still plague the collector: they become progressively more difficult to identify, especially as many have been around long enough to acquire a decently 'worn' look. The range of rare badges now available as re-strikes grows annually, and new collectors would be well advised to limit their purchases of such items to well established dealers prepared to back their sales with some form of guarantee.

As always I am again indebted to Laurie Archer for his invaluable assistance.
                                                                                 F. W., 1983

Note: when using the following price guide, the reader is advised to bear in mind the Notes and Corrections to be found immediately preceding the index.

# PRICE GUIDE

1. 80th Regiment of Foot, *c.* 1850: £120.
2. 9th (The East Norfolk) Regiment of Foot, *c.* 1820: £140.
3. 17th (Leicestershire) Regiment of Foot, *c.* 1800: £120.
4. Officer, King's Own 2nd Staffordshire Militia, *c.* 1840: £100.
5. 86th (Royal County Down) Regiment of Foot, *c.* 1850: £100.
6. Helmet plate, Territorial Royal Artillery, 1902–22: £45.
7. Helmet plate, Royal Warwickshire Regiment, 1881–1901: £40 (but note back plate is post 1953).
8. Helmet plate, The Queen's (Royal West Surrey) Regiment, post 1902: £45.
9. Helmet plate, North Staffordshire Regiment, 1881–1902: £40 (but note back plate is post 1953).
10. Officer's helmet plate, Middlesex Regiment, post 1902: £100.
11. Shako plate of Tower Hamlets, pre 1901: £65.
12. Gilt plate, Royal Military College, Sandhurst, pre 1901: £30 (but this may be officer's pouch plate of Army Medical Staff).
13. Officer's belt buckle, Engineer Volunteers, *c.* 1860: £45.
14. 34th (Cumberland) Regiment, 1860–81: £55.
15. Cypher from a sabretache: £12.
16. Leicestershire Yeomanry Cavalry, fitting from sabretache: £20 (from pouch).
17. King's Royal Rifle Corps, 1881–1901: £20.
18. N.C.O.'s arm badge, 17th (Duke of Cambridge's Own) Lancers, pre 1922: £20.
19. Helmet plate, West Meath Rifle Regiment, pre 1881: £125.
20. 6th Dragoon Guard (Carabiniers), pre 1901: £25.
21. 4th (Queen's Own) Hussars, pre 1901: £30.
22. Shako plate, 95th Regiment of Foot. 1861–69: £80.
23. Glengarry badge, 93rd Regiment of Foot, 1879–81: £65.
24. Officer's shako plate, 2nd Queen's Regiment, 1861–69 (with silver centre): £90.
25. The King's Royal Rifle Corps, 1881–1901: £18.
26. Glengarry badge, Dublin County Light Infantry, post 1881: £50 (more if hallmarked silver).
27. Officer's glengarry badge, Worcester Regiment, 1881–98 (gilt with silver centre): £65.
28. South Staffordshire Regiment, pre 1901: £30 (white metal).
29. Sergeant, Scots Guards: £12.
30. Scots Guards: £5.
31. Officer's glengarry badge, Royal Inniskilling Fusiliers, post 1881: £60.
32. Officer, Scots Guards: £20.
33. Collar badge, The Royal Norfolk Regiment: £3.
34, 35. Pair of collar badges, The Royal Warwickshire Regiment: £6.
36. General officer's cap badge: £10.
37. Collar badge, The Highland Light Infantry: £3.
38. Sergeant's arm badge, Royal Artillery: £3.
39. Collar badge, The Gordon Highlanders: £6 a pair. See 41.
40. Puggaree badge, the King's Own Yorkshire Light Infantry: £20.
41. As 39.
42. Queen's Own Oxfordshire Hussars, pre 1901: £15.
43. Royal Irish Rifles, pre 1902: £50.
44. Volunteer, Lancashire Fusiliers: £38.
45. 18th Hussars, pre 1902: £22.
46. Glengarry badge, black, 4th Surrey Rifle Volunteer Corps, pre 1901: £45.
47. Glengarry badge, black, 3rd Volunteer Battalion, East Surrey Regiment, pre 1901: £45.
48. Black Watch, pre 1901: £16.
49. 13th Hussars, bi-metal, pre 1901: £24.
50. Derbyshire Regiment (Sherwood Foresters), pre 1901: £16.
51. Grenadier Guards: £4.
52. Warrant Officer, Orderly Room Sergeant and Band Sergeant, Grenadier Guards: £14 (crown and cypher laid on).
53. First Life Guards: £10.
54. Household Cavalry (Elizabeth II): £4.
55. The Royal Horse Guards (The Blues): £4.
56. Coldstream Guards: £4.
57. Welsh Guards: £4.
58. Irish Guards: £4.
59. The Life Guards (George VI): £7.
60. Second Life Guards (George V): £10.
61. Royal Armoured Corps, post 1939: £6.
62. Royal Armoured Corps (Elizabeth II): £4.
63. Collar badge, Tank Corps: £3.
64. Royal Tank Regiment (1922–39 Royal Tank Corps): £4.
65. Tank Corps, 1917: £9.
66. Sleeve badge, Tank Corps, 1917: £12.
67. 1st King's Dragoon Guards, 1915–37: £12. (£8 if bi-metal).
68. 4th Royal Irish Dragoon Guards: £14 (£10 if bi-metal).
69. Second Dragoon Guards (Queen's Bays): £7.
70. 1st King's Dragoon Guards, post 1938: £12 (more if hallmarked silver).
71. 5th Dragoon Guards, 1902–22: £15 (£12 if bi-metal).
72. 3rd Dragoon Guards: £15 (£12 if bi-metal).
73. 1st (King's) Dragoon Guards with scroll (1898–1915): £16
74. 1st (King's) Dragoon Guards, post 1938: £9 (£6 if white metal).
75. 4th/7th Royal Dragoon Guards, post 1922: £6.

76. 1st Royal Dragoons, post 1936: £8.
77. 6th Dragoon Guards (Carabiniers), 1902–22: £10 (£14 if gilding metal).
78. 7th Dragoon Guards, 1898–1906: £13.
79. 3rd Carabiniers (Prince of Wales' Dragoon Guards), post 1922: £6.
80. The Royal Scots Greys (2nd Dragoons): £6.
81. 3rd King's Own Hussars: £5.
82. 1st Royal Dragoons, 1902–36: £8.
83. 7th Queen's Own Hussars: 1902–58: £7.
84. 4th Queen's Own Hussars: 1907–58: £7.
85. 8th King's Irish Hussars: £8.
86. 9th Queen's Royal Lancers: £9.
87. 11th Hussars (Prince Albert's Own):£7.
88. 5th Royal Irish Lancers: £20.
89. 6th Inniskilling Dragoons: £14.
90. 10th Royal Hussars: £7.
91. 15th (King's) Hussars: £16.
92. 14th (King's) Hussars: £16.
93. 19th Hussars: £12.
94. 18th (Queen Mary's Own) Hussars, 1911–22: £12.
95. 12th Lancers: £9.
96. 17th/21st Lancers, post 1922: £6.
97. 13th Hussars, 1901–22: £16.
98. 16th (The Queen's) Lancers: £10.
99. 21st (Empress of India) Lancers: £20 (£15 if bi-metal).
100. 20th Hussars: £12.
101. 24th Lancers: £12.
102. 27th Lancers: £15.
103. 23rd Hussars: £8.
104. 21st Lancers (points and butts of lances missing): £125 (if complete).
105. 5th Royal Inniskilling Dragoon Guards: £7.
106. Reconnaissance Corps, disbanded 1946: £5.
107. Royal Wiltshire Yeomanry: £7.
108. The Queen's Own Hussars: £3.
109. 9th/12th Royal Lancers: £3.
110. North Irish Horse: £9.
111. Fife and Forfar Yeomanry: £6.
112. Officer's badge, Scottish Horse: £16.
113. Welsh Horse: £10.
114. 13th/18th Royal Hussars: £7.
115. 14th (King's) Hussars, 1898–1915: £14 (£18 if gilding metal).
116. 15th/19th The King's Royal Hussars, post 1922: £9.
117. South Irish Horse: £10.
118. 14th/20th King's Hussars: £8.
119. 14th/20th King's Hussars with 'FR' on chest: £60.
120. Forage cap badge, 13th Hussars, post 1902: £25.
121. The Queen's Own Cameron Highlanders: £5.
122. The Royal Scots: £5.
123. The Liverpool Scottish: 1937–69: £8.
124. The London Scottish: £8.
125. The King's Own Scottish Borderers: £5.
126. 10th (Scottish) Battalion, The King's (Liverpool) Regiment, 1908–37: £12.
127. The Gordon Highlanders: £5.
128. The Cameronians (Scottish Rifles): £5.

129. Royal Scots Fusiliers: £7.
130. The Black Watch (Royal Highland Regiment): £6.
131. The Highland Light Infantry (City of Glasgow Regiment): £5.
132. Lovat Scouts: £6.
133. Argyll and Sutherland Highlanders: £5.
134. Lowland Regiment: £12.
135. The Glasgow Highlanders (The Highland Light Infantry): £8.
136. The Black Watch: £6.
137. Lanarkshire Yeomanry, 1955–6: £10.
138. Seaforth Highlanders: £5.
139. Ayrshire (Earl of Carrick's Own) Yeomanry: £7.
140. The Lowland Brigade: £4.
141. Highland Brigade: £4.
142. 5th Battn. Seaforth Highlanders: 1908–20: £16.
143. Tyneside Scottish: £12.
144. 8th (Irish) Battn. The King's Regiment (Liverpool): £12.
145. Connaught Rangers: £15.
146. Royal Munster Fusiliers: £16.
147. The Leinster Regiment: £16.
148. The Royal Ulster Rifles: £4.
149. Royal Dublin Fusiliers: £16.
150, 150a. Royal Irish Fusiliers, £8.
151. Dublin National Volunteers: £15.
152. The Royal Irish Regiment: £15.
153. The Royal Fusiliers: £4.
154. The Buffs (Royal East Kent Regiment): £4.
155. Royal Northumberland Fusiliers: 1935–60: £5.
156. The King's Own Royal Regiment (Lancaster): £4.
157. Northumberland Fusiliers, pre 1935: £6.
158. The Queen's (Royal West Surrey Regiment): £6.
159. Royal Warwickshire Regiment: £4.
160. The Royal Lincolnshire Regiment, post 1946: £8.
161. The Lincolnshire Regiment: £4.
162. The Norfolk Regiment, pre 1935: £7.
163. The Devonshire Regiment: £4.
164. Beret, The Royal Norfolk Regiment: £6.
165. The Royal Norfolk Regiment, 1935–60: £4.
166. The King's Regiment (Liverpool): pre 1926: £7.
167. The King's Regiment (Liverpool): 1926–60: £4.
168. The Suffolk Regiment, 1915–19: £9.
169. The East Yorkshire Regiment, 1915–19: £9.
170. West Yorkshire Regiment: £4.
171. The East Yorkshire Regiment: £4.
172. West Yorkshire Regiment: £4.
173. The Suffolk Regiment: £4.
174. Bronze collar badge, West Yorkshire Regiment: £2.
175. 4th Battn. The Somerset Light Infantry: £10.
176. The Somerset Light Infantry (Prince Albert's): £4.

177. The Green Howards (Alexandra Princess of Wales' Own Yorkshire Regiment), 1908–1951: £6.
178. The Green Howards (Alexandra Princess of Wales' Own Yorkshire Regiment), 1908–51: £4.
179. The Green Howards (Alexandra Princess of Wales' Own Yorkshire Regiment), 1951–60: £6.
180. The Green Howards (Alexandra Princess of Wales' Own Yorkshire Regiment), 1915–19: £9.
181. The Bedfordshire Regiment: pre 1915: £24.
182. The Leicestershire Regiment: £4.
183. The Bedfordshire Regiment: pre 1915: £6.
184. The Hertfordshire Regiment: £5.
185. The Royal Leicestershire Regiment, post 1946: £6.
186. The Bedfordshire Regiment, 1915–19: £9.
187. The Bedfordshire and Hertfordshire Regiment: post 1919: £4.
188. The Royal Welsh Fusiliers, 1915–19: £10.
189. The Lancashire Fusiliers: £5.
190. Royal Welsh Fusiliers: post 1920: £5.
191. The South Wales Borderers: £5.
192. The Devonshire Regiment: £12.
193. The Cheshire Regiment, post 1922: £4.
194. The Cheshire Regiment, 1898–1922: £6.
195. The Royal Inniskilling Fusiliers, post 1934: £7.
196. The Worcestershire Regiment, pre 1925: £7.
197. The Worcestershire Regiment, 1925–66: £4.
198. The East Lancashire Regiment: £4.
199. The East Lancashire Regiment: £14 (militia).
200. The East Lancashire Regiment: 1915–19: £9.
201. The Gloucestershire Regiment: £5.
202. The Gloucestershire Regiment: £4.
203. The Gloucestershire Regiment. £14.
204. The Duke of Wellington's Regiment (West Riding): £4.
205. The East Surrey Regiment: £4.
206. The Border Regiment, post 1953: £4.
207. The Border Regiment, 1915–19: £15.
208. The Duke of Cornwall's Light Infantry: £4.
209. The East Surrey Regiment, 1915–19: £8.
210. The East Surrey Regiment: £15.
211. The Dorsetshire Regiment: £4.
212. The South Staffordshire Regiment, £4.
213. The Royal Hampshire Regiment: £8.
214. The Hampshire Regiment, pre 1946: £4.
215. The Royal Sussex Regiment: £4.
216. The Hampshire Regiment, officer's pattern: £6.
217. The Hampshire Regiment, officer's pattern: £6.
218. 5th (Cinque Ports) Battn. Royal Sussex Regiment: £12.
219. The Welch Regiment: £5.
220. The Welsh Regiment, pre 1920: £6.
221. The Welsh Regiment, pre 1920: £16 (scarce in white metal).
222. The South Lancashire (Prince of Wales' Volunteers): £4.
223. The Essex Regiment: £4.
224. Volunteer badge, The Essex Regiment: £10.
225. The South Lancashire (Prince of Wales' Volunteers): £7.
226. The Oxfordshire and Buckinghamshire Light Infantry: £6.
227. The Oxfordshire and Buckinghamshire Light Infantry: £4.
228. Royal Marine Artillery: £12.
229. 7th (The Robin Hoods) Battn. Nottinghamshire and Derbyshire Regiment: £10.
230. The Royal Berkshire Regiment: £4.
231. The Sherwood Foresters (Nottinghamshire and Derbyshire Regiment): £4.
232. The Royal Marine Light Infantry: £9.
233. The Royal Marines: £4.
234. The Northamptonshire Regiment: £12.
235. The Royal West Kent Regiment: £4.
236. The Loyal North Lancashire Regiment, 1902–20: £6.
237. The Middlesex Regiment: £4.
238. The King's Shropshire Light Infantry: £4.
239. The Manchester Regiment: £6.
240. The King's Own Yorkshire Light Infantry: £5.
241. The King's Royal Rifle Corps: £4.
242. The King's Shropshire Light Infantry, beret: £6.
243. Officer's badge (The Middlesex Regiment): £6.
244. The Manchester Regiment, pre 1923: £7.
245. The Wiltshire Regiment: £4.
246. The York and Lancaster Regiment: £4.
247. 6th Battn. The Durham Light Infantry: £7.
248. The Durham Light Infantry: £4.
249. The Rifle Brigade, 1911–34: £7.
250. The Rifle Brigade (Prince Consort's Own), 1934–58. £6.
251. The Loyal Regiment, 1920–53: £6.
252. The North Staffordshire Regiment: £4.
253. The North Staffordshire Regiment, 1915–19: £9.
254. The Royal Air Force: £4.
255. The Army Air Corps, 1942–50: £9.
256. The Royal Flying Corps: £9.
257. The Royal Artillery: £3.
258. The Parachute Regiment: £6.
259. The Honourable Artillery Company: £10.
260. The Honourable Artillery Company, beret: £6.
261. The Royal Artillery, beret: £3.
262. Officer's badge, The Royal Artillery Territorial Force: £10.
263. The 21st S.A.S. Artists Rifles: £6.
264. Dress Busby Badge, Royal Air Force: £65.
265. The Royal Army Service Corps, post 1953: £3.
266. The Royal Army Service Corps, post 1953: £2 (anodised).

267. The Royal Army Medical Corps: £3.
268. Royal Army Chaplains Department: £10 (black).
269. S.A.S. Regiment: £2 (anodised).
270. The Army Veterinary Corps, 1903–18: £10.
271. The Army Service Corps, 1914–18: £6.
272. Royal Army Service Corps, George VI: £3.
273. Royal Army Dental Corps: £4.
274. Army Pay Corps, 1902–20: £10.
275. Queen Alexandra's Royal Army Nursing Corps, 1949–54: £8.
276. The Royal Corps of Signals: £3.
277. The Royal Army Pay Corps, 1920–29: £35.
278. Royal Electrical and Mechanical Engineers, 1942–47: £3.
279. Royal Corps of Signals: £4.
280. Royal Electrical and Mechanical Engineers, 1947–53: £3.
281. Army Dental Corps, 1921–46: £8.
282. Army Pay Corps: £12.
283. Royal Army Pay Corps, 1929–53: £3.
284. Army Educational Corps, 1920–46: £10.
285. The Royal Pioneer Corps: £3.
286. The Royal Army Educational Corps, post 1953: £3.
287. Norfolk Yeomanry: £10.
288. The Royal Pioneer Corps: £3.
289. Royal Military Police, post 1953: £3.
290. Corps of Military Police, George VI: £5.
291. Royal Army Ordnance Corps: 1949–53: £5.
292. Women's Legion: £10.
293. Women's Royal Army Corps, 1949–53: £3.
294. Army Ordnance Corps, pre 1920: £7.
295. Auxiliary Territorial Service: £3.
296. Army Remount Service: £14.
297. Royal Army Ordnance Corps, 1920–47: £3.
298. Royal Army Ordnance Corps with motto, 1947–49: £7.
299. Militia badge, Honourable Artillery Company: £6.
300. Warrant officer's cap badge, Honourable Artillery Company: £15.
301. Royal Horse Artillery: £6.
302. Army Physical Training Corps: £10.
303. Machine Gun Corps: £6.
304. Army Catering Corps: £3.
305. Intelligence Corps: £5.
306. Junior Leaders Training Regiment: £3.
307. Queen's Royal Surrey Regiment: £4.
308. Officer's badge, East Anglia Regiment (silver and gilt): £9.
309. Queen's Regiment: post 1966: £2.
310. Small Arms School Corps, post 1929: £12.
311. Royal Military Academy, Woolwich: £10.
312. Royal Military Academy, Sandhurst: £9.
313. National Defence Company: £8.
314. Royal Military College, Sandhurst: £10.
315. 3rd County of London Yeomanry (The Sharpshooters): £8.
316. The City of London Yeomanry (Rough Riders): £18.

317. 3rd/4th County of London Yeomanry (Sharpshooters): £10.
318. Army Cyclist Corps: £6.
319. Inns of Court O.T.C.: £6.
320. King Edward's Horse (The King's Overseas Dominions Regiment): £12.
321. Westminster Dragoons: £7.
322. 2nd King Edward's Horse: £9.
323. Inns of Court Regiment, pre 1961: £6.
324. 5th City of London Regiment (London Rifle Brigade): £7.
325. 10th London Regiment (Hackney), post 1912: £7.
326. 5th City of London Regiment: £10.
327. Royal Fusiliers (City of London Regiment): £4.
328. 5th City of London Regiment Cadets: £6.
329. 7th City of London Regiment: £12.
330. 10th County of London Regiment (Paddington Rifles), 1908–12: £40.
331. 11th London Regiment (Finsbury Rifles): £10.
332. 8th Battn. City of London Regiment (Post Office Rifles): £10.
333. 9th London Regiment (Queen Victoria's Rifles): £10.
334. 18th London Regiment (London Irish Rifles): £10.
335. Queen's Royal Rifles: £7.
336. 19th London Regiment (St. Pancras): £10.
337. 15th London Regiment (Prince of Wales' Own Civil Service Rifles): £10.
338. 12th London Regiment (Rangers): £12.
339. 23rd London Regiment (The East Surrey Regiment): £10.
340. 16th County of London (Queen's Westminsters), pre 1921: £9.
341. 16th London Regiment (Queen's Westminsters and Civil Service Rifles), post 1921: £9.
342. 25th County of London (Cyclists): £10.
343. 28th London Regiment (Artists' Rifles): £7.
344. 13th London Regiment (Princess Louise's Kensington Regiment): £6.
345. 24th London Regiment (The Queen's): £4.
346. Officer, 20th London Regiment (The Queen's Own): £10.
347. The Queen's Own Yorkshire Yeomanry, 1956–69: £7.
348. The Queen's Own Worcestershire Hussars: £10.
349. The Warwickshire Yeomanry: £3.
350. The Cambridgeshire Regiment: £7.
351. East Riding Yeomanry: £7.
352. Yorkshire Dragoons (Queen's Own), black: £6.
353. Yorkshire Hussars (Alexandra Princess of Wales' Own): £7.
354. The Lothian and Border Horse: £6.
355. Duke of Lancaster's Own Yeomanry: £8.
356. The Lothian and Border Horse, with tie and stalks: £6.
357. Leicestershire Yeomanry (Prince Albert's Own): £7.

358. North Somerset Yeomanry: £8.
359. Shropshire Yeomanry: £8.
360. Cheshire (Earl of Chester's) Yeomanry: £8.
361. Duke of Lancaster's Own Yeomanry: £7.
362. 5th Battn. Border Regiment: £18.
363. The Westmorland and Cumberland Yeomanry: £18.
364. The Pembroke Yeomanry: £12.
365. The Royal East Kent Yeomanry: £7.
366. The South Nottinghamshire Hussars: £7.
367. The Northumberland Hussars: £7.
368. The Northamptonshire Yeomanry: £8.
369. The Hampshire Yeomanry (Carabiniers): £7.
370. The West Somerset Yeomanry: £10.
371. The Royal Devon Yeomanry Artillery: £7.
372. The Royal Buckinghamshire Hussars: £7.
373. The Queen's Own Dorset Yeomanry, 1902–18: £12.
374. The Queen's Own Dorset Yeomanry, post 1920: £10.
375. The Berkshire Yeomanry: £7.
376. The Berkshire Imperial Yeomanry: £25.
377. The Glamorgan Yeomanry: £12.
378. The Lancashire Hussars (Imperial Yeomanry): £25.
379. The Essex Yeomanry: £7.
380. The Sussex Yeomanry: £7.
381. The Norfolk Yeomanry (The King's Own Regiment): £8.
382. The Surrey Yeomanry: £7.
383. 1st Battn. Monmouthshire Regiment: £8.
348. 2nd Battn. Monmouthshire Regiment: £7.
385. Norfolk Yeomanry: £14.
386. The Lincolnshire Yeomanry: £10.
387. The Leeds Rifles (Cockburn High School Cadets): £12.
388. The Herefordshire Light Infantry: £7.
389. 8th Battn. P.W.O. West Yorkshire Regiment (Leeds Rifles): £12.
390. The Herefordshire Regiment: £7.
391. The Loyal Suffolk Hussars: £7.
392. 7th/8th Bttn. P.W.O. West Yorkshire Regiment (Leeds Rifles): £8.
393. 6th Battn. Hampshire (Duke of Connaught's Own): £7.
394. Middlesex Imperial Yeomanry: £20.
395. Officer's badge, Yorkshire Brigade: £10.
396. Tyneside Irish, 1914–19: £16.
397. Huntingdonshire Home Guard: £10.
398. The Buckinghamshire Battn. (Oxfordshire and Buckinghamshire Light Infantry): £6.
399. The Mobile Defence Corps: £5.
400. Royal Observer Corps: £6.
401. The Princess of Wales' Own Yorkshire Regiment, 1902–8: £18.
402. Royal Militia: £10.
403. Royal Malta Militia shako: £25.
404. Imperial Yeomanry slouch hat with rosette: £35.
405. Royal Malta Artillery beret: £4.
406. Sharpshooters: £30.
407. Royal Malta Artillery: £5.
408. Army Scripture Readers: £30.
409. School of Musketry: £18.
410. Royal Engineers: £6.
411. National Defence Company: £15.
412. Royal Engineers (George VI): £4.
413. Royal Engineers (Elizabeth II): £3.
414. Royal Engineers (George V, 1910–35): £3.
415. Royal Engineers (Edward VII): £10.
416. Royal Engineers (George V, 1915–19): £7.

# BADGES OF THE BRITISH ARMY

## 1820–1960

# BADGES OF THE BRITISH ARMY

# 1820–1960

An Illustrated Reference Guide

for Collectors

*by*

F. WILKINSON

ARMS AND ARMOUR PRESS

Published by
Arms and Armour Press, Lionel Leventhal Limited,
2–6 Hampstead High Street, London NW3 1QQ
Australia: 4–12 Tattersalls Lane, Melbourne, Victoria 3000
South Africa: Sanso Centre, 8 Adderley Street,
P.O. Box 94, Cape Town 8000
United States of America: Cameron and Kelker Streets,
P.O. Box 1831, Harrisburg, Pa. 17105
Canada: Fortress Publications Inc., P.O. Box 241,
Stoney Creek, Ontario 18G 3X9



First edition 1969
Second edition, revised, 1971
Second impression 1972
Third impression 1976
Third edition, with Price Guide Supplement, 1978
Fourth edition, with Price Guide Supplement, 1980
Fifth edition, with Price Guide Supplement, 1982
Sixth edition, with Price Guide Supplement, 1984

*British Library Cataloguing in Publication Data*
Wilkinson, Frederick
Badges of the British Army, 1820–1960. – 6th ed.
1. Great Britain. *Army* – Medals, badges, decorations, etc. –
Pictorial Works I. Title
355.1′4  UC535.G7
ISBN 0-85368-629-7

Printed in Great Britain
by Fletcher & Son Ltd, Norwich

# INTRODUCTION

AFTER many years of comparative anarchy, British Army uniforms were at last beginning to acquire a degree of standardisation by the late seventeenth century, and from the mid eighteenth century official regulations, known as clothing warrants, were formulated which specified the general details of the dress. Prior to 1751 almost all regiments were identified by the name of their commanding colonel, but in that year each was given a number; many regiments also had a name—thus the 27th Regiment was also known as the Inniskilling Regiment. The practice of using numbers and names became commonplace and many regiments were given the right to use, as an identifying emblem, a device which commemorated some special battle, a campaign or other regimental association. Name, number and device, together or in various combinations, came increasingly to be placed on buttons, buckles and head-dress. In the early eighteenth century badges were mostly embroidered on the mitre caps of the Grenadiers but by the latter part of the century metal plates bearing regimental names or devices were introduced. These were at first fairly basic, being a simple strip bearing the name, but by the early nineteenth century they were large and more detailed.

Size and shape of these badges were obviously influenced by the particular form of head-dress worn and with the tall 'stovepipe' shako of the early nineteenth century the badge was a fairly large, die-stamped, metal plate. For the Waterloo shako the badge was still stamped out of brass for other ranks but was a little smaller than the previous type. In 1829 a bell-topped shako was adopted and with this style of head-dress was introduced the 'star' pattern badge; this basic form was to be used by most regiments, with but a few breaks, continuously until the present day. The Albert Shako also used a large 'star badge' with the regimental devices applied to the main plate. However in 1855, a lower crowned shako was adopted and needed a correspondingly smaller badge. The large pattern 'star' badge was reintroduced in 1879 when the so-called blue-cloth helmet was adopted by the British Army. Smaller badges were again in style when the service dress cap came into use in the early twentieth century and even smaller varieties were worn on the beret which was first used during the 1914-18 war. Special badges were made for the Glengarry cap which was introduced in 1874 and for fitting to the puggaree (spelt in a variety of ways!) worn wrapped around the tropical helmet. The great majority of badges illustrated in this book are those intended for the cap and beret although a number of shako and glengarry examples, as well as helmet plates, are included.

Although much has been written on the history of badges in general and regiments in particular, there are still many gaps in our knowledge. Variations on a basic theme are numerous and in many cases these are no more than minor differences owing to different dies being used by the manufacturers; but many others are far less easily explained. Official publications, such as the Dress Regulations, are not as definitive as one might expect; thus, in the issue of 1883 the badge of the Norfolk Regiment is described as 'The Figure of Britannia in Silver' – hardly sufficient to identify a badge as being of that date. It must also be remembered that the published regulations only referred to the dress of officers. Often there are no surviving records of the badges worn by certain battalions and it is difficult, if not impossible, to date some badges with certainty. Further confusion is introduced by the fact that other badges, often almost identical with those on the cap, were worn on the sleeve and on the collar. It is often difficult to distinguish one from another.

Whilst it is usually not difficult to allocate any badge to its regiment, dating is a very different matter. There are, however, a few obvious pointers which are valid in making broad divisions. During Queen Victoria's reign the crown used on badges had arms which curled up, over and down again – the type referred to by collectors as the 'Queen's Crown' (see numbers 11, 12, 14, 15 etc.). When Edward VII ascended the throne in 1901 the pattern was changed to that on numbers 53, 59, 60 etc. On the accession of Elizabeth II in 1953 the crown was altered to one very similar to that of Victoria (see numbers 55, 62 etc.). Thus a great majority of badges can easily be allocated as pre or post 1901. There are exceptions which must be mentioned and they are the badges of regiments such as the Green Howards (Alexandra, Princess of Wales' Own Yorkshire Regiment, badge numbers 177–180) which incorporate foreign crowns. A further obvious distinction can be made with the majority of British Army badges since, as the result of recommendations made by the Stanley Committee in 1877, a complete reorganisation was undertaken in 1881 and regiments lost their numbers and were given a name, usually that of a county or town. At the same time a number of regiments were amalgamated, a process repeated at intervals up to the present. The change of title offers yet another broad dating and the details of such changes may be found in such books as 'Records and Badges of Every Regiment and Corps in the British Army' by H. M. Chichester and G. Burgess-Short (reprinted, London, 1970), 'Lineage Book of the British Army' by J. Frederick (1969), 'Shoulder-Belt Plates and Buttons' by H. Parkyn (1956). It must be borne in mind that cavalry regiments did not lose their numbers and retain them today.

Brass, a versatile metal, has long been used for the manufacture of badges and buttons, especially for the use of other ranks; for officers silver and gilt were the most common materials. White metal has also been used in the manufacture of badges, especially those of the militia and Scottish regiments, and many overseas Scottish units, particularly those of Canada, have followed this practice. Some badges combine both materials, having a brass badge with white metal scroll or emblem – these are referred to as bi-metal. During World War II when metal was in short supply plastics were used for badges and later a permanent shiny surface was applied. Another variety of badge, usually known as Officers Service Dress, is of a matt, bronze colour. In this book all badges illustrated are of brass unless otherwise indicated by W.M. (white metal) or BI (bi-metal) and are for other ranks, again unless otherwise indicated. (It must also be pointed out that examples in materials other than the one illustrated may be encountered – it was virtually impossible to include all versions.)

Collecting badges is one of the very few hobbies left open for the collector of modest means; most badges cost only a few shillings and rare ones only a few pounds. Interest has grown enormously over the last few years or so and it has become much less easy to find specimens; however, a number of reputable dealers have taken up the sale of badges and their lists are always worth having.

Despite the greater demand it is still possible for the collector to discover a 'treasure' and it is this hope that helps keep a collector happy and interested.


## ACKNOWLEDGEMENTS

With few exceptions all the badges in this book are from the extensive collection of Jim Burgess. He disarranged his entire collection in order to make this selection and gave of his time and knowledge generously and cheerfully. It is no more than the truth to say that without him there would have been no book and I most gratefully acknowledge my indebtedness.

Since this work was published a number of people have pointed out errors and omissions—although it must be said that agreement was by no means unanimous. A list of these notes and corrections appears at the end of the plates. Amongst those whose help is gratefully acknowledged are Hugh King, Roy Butler of Wallis and Wallis, and Laurence V. Archer.

Special thanks are due to Gary Williams who compiled a comprehensive index and this, with slight modifications, has been added in this revised edition as a most useful aid to reference and identification.

Shoulder-Belt Plates. **1.** 80th Regiment of Foot, later united with the 38th to form The South Staffordshire Regiment. 2½″ x 3½″, *c.*1850. **2.** 9th (The East Norfolk) Regiment of Foot, later The Norfolk Regiment. 2½″ x 3½″, *c.*1820. **3.** 17th (Leicestershire) Regiment of Foot, from 1881 The Leicestershire Regiment. 3¾″ x 3″, *c.*1800. **4.** Officer, King's Own 2nd Staffordshire Militia. Silver and brass. 3″ x 3¾″, *c.*1840. **5.** 86th (Royal County Down) Regiment of Foot which in 1881 was formed into The Royal Irish Rifles. 2¾″ x 3½″, *c.*1850.

**6**. Helmet Plate, Royal Artillery, post 1902.  **7**. Helmet Plate, Royal Warwickshire Regiment, 1881–1901.  **8**. Helmet Plate, The Queen's (Royal West Surrey) Regiment, post 1902.  **9**. Helmet Plate, North Staffordshire Regiment, 1881–1902.  **10**. Officer's Helmet Plate, Middlesex Regiment.  Gilt and silver, post 1902.

11. Shako plate of Tower Hamlets, later 17th London Regiment. W.M., pre 1901.
12. Gilt plate, Royal Military College, Sandhurst, pre 1901.   13. Officer's belt buckle,
Engineer Volunteers. Silver with gilt centre, c. 1860.   14. 34th (Cumberland) Regiment,
later part of The Border Regiment. Brass badge, 1860–81.   15. White metal cypher
from a sabretache.   16. Leicestershire Yeomanry Cavalry.   White metal fitting from
sabretache.

**17.** King's Royal Rifle Corps, 1881–1901.  **18.** N.C.O. arm badge, 17th (Duke of Cambridge's Own) Lancers.  Unusual as nose cavity pierces plate.  Silver, pre 1922. **19.** Helmet plate, West Meath Rifle Regiment, cross of W.M., pre 1881.  **20.** 6th Dragoon Guard (Carabiniers), pre 1901.  **21.** 4th (Queen's Own) Hussars, pre 1901.

22. Helmet plate, 95th (The Derbyshire) Regiment of Foot, later 2nd Battn. Derbyshire Regiment (The Sherwood Foresters), pre 1881.  23. Badge of 93rd Regiment of Foot (Sutherland Highlanders).  24. Helmet plate, 2nd Queen's (Royal West Surrey) Regiment.  25. The King's Royal Rifle Corps, 1881–1901.  26. Dublin County Light Infantry. Silver, pre 1881.  27. Worcester Regiment, pre 1901.  28. South Staffordshire Regiment, pre 1901.

29. Sergeant, Scots Guards, BI.   30. Scots Guards.   31. Royal Inniskilling Fusiliers.
32. Officer, Scots Guards.   33. Collar badge, The Royal Norfolk Regiment.   34,35.
Pair of collar badges, The Royal Warwickshire Regiment, W.M.   36. General Officer's
cap badge.   37. Collar badge, The Highland Light Infantry, W.M.   38. Sergeant's Arm
Badge, Royal Artillery.   One of a pair worn muzzles to the front.   39. Collar badge,
The Gordon Highlanders, W.M.   40. Forage Cap and Puggaree, The King's Own
Yorkshire Light Infantry.   41. As 39.

42. Queen's Own Oxfordshire Hussars.  Silver, pre 1901.  **43**. Royal Irish Rifles. Silver, pre 1902.  **44**. Lancashire Fusiliers, W.M.  **45**. 18th Hussars, pre 1902.  **46**. 4th Surrey Rifle Volunteer Corps, pre 1901.  **47**. 3rd Volunteer Battalion, East Surrey Regiment, pre 1901.  **48**. Black Watch, W.M., pre 1901.  **49**. 13th Hussars, BI, pre 1901.  **50**. Derbyshire Regiment (Sherwood Foresters), pre 1901.

51. Grenadier Guards.   52. Warrant Officer, Orderly Room Sergeant and Band Sergeant, Grenadier Guards. 53. First Life Guards. 54. Household Cavalry (Elizabeth II). 55. The Royal Horse Guards (The Blues). 56. Coldstream Guards. 57. Welsh Guards. 58. Irish Guards. 59. The Life Guards (George VI). 60. Second Life Guards (George V).

61. Royal Armoured Corps, post 1939. 62. Royal Armoured Corps (Elizabeth II), W.M. 63. Collar badge, Tank Corps. 64. Royal Tank Regiment (1922–39 Royal Tank Corps). 65. Tank Corps, 1917. 66. Sleeve badge, Tank Corps, 1917.

**67.** 1st King's Dragoon Guards, 1915–37. **68.** 4th Royal Irish Dragoon Guards. **69.** Second Dragoon Guards (Queen's Bays). **70.** 1st King's Dragoon Guards. Silver, post 1938. **71.** 5th Dragoon Guards, 1902–22. **72.** 3rd Dragoon Guards. **73.** 1st (King's) Dragoon Guards with scroll, (1898–1915). **74.** 1st (King's) Dragoon Guards, post 1938.

75. 4th/7th Royal Dragoon Guards, post 1922.  76. 1st Royal Dragoons, post 1936.
77. 6th Dragoon Guards (Carabiniers), 1902–22, (*cf.* 20).  78. 7th Dragoon Guards,
1898–1906.  79. 3rd Carabiniers (Prince of Wales' Dragoon Guards), post 1922.
80. The Royal Scots Greys (2nd Dragoons), BI.  81. 3rd King's Own Hussars, BI.
82. 1st Royal Dragoons, 1902–36.

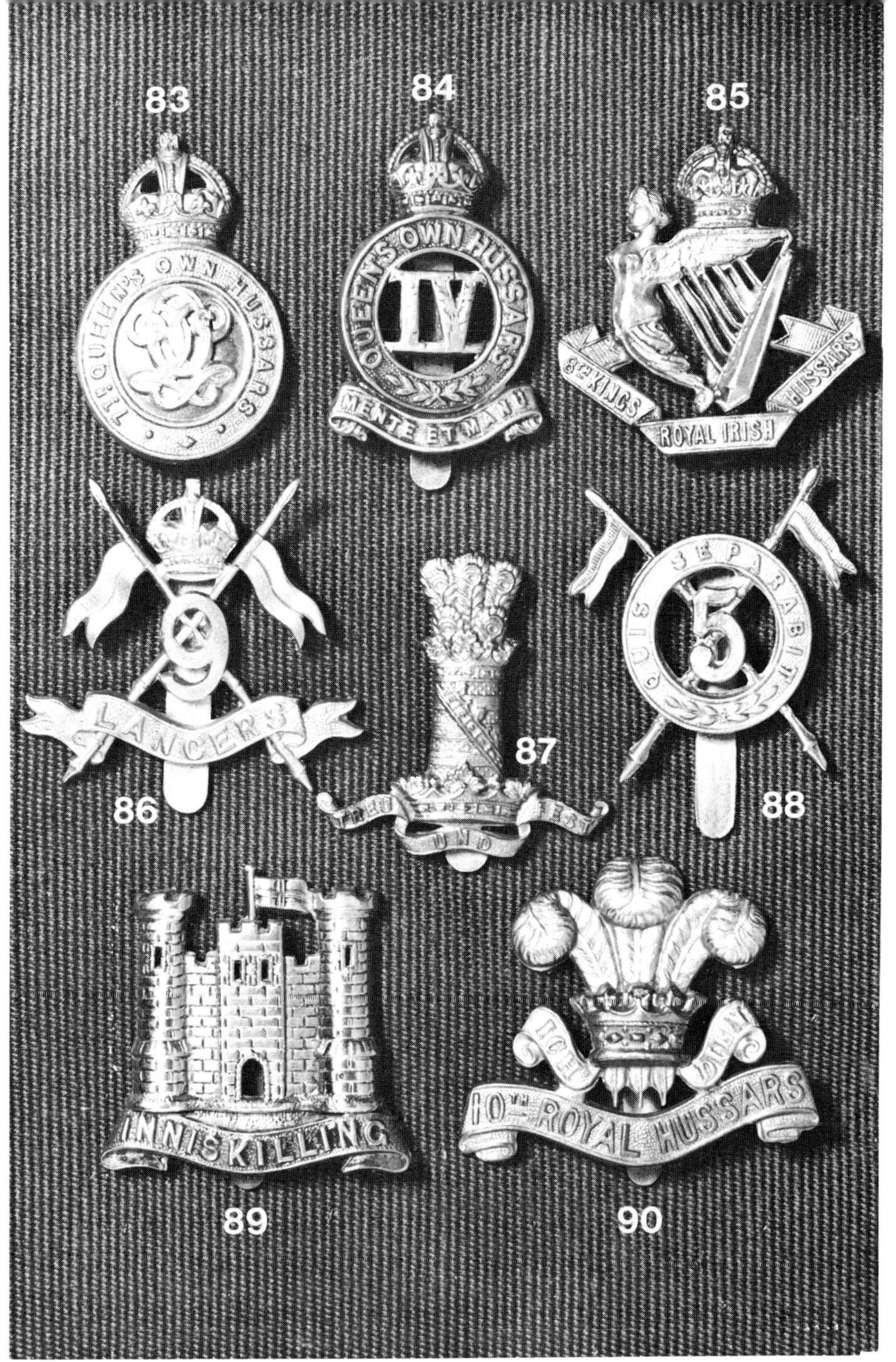

83. 7th Queen's Own Hussars, BI, 1902–58.  84. 4th Queen's Own Hussars, BI, 1907–58.  85. 8th King's Royal Irish Hussars.  86. 9th Queen's Royal Lancers, W.M. 87. 11th Hussars (Prince Albert's Own).  88. 5th Royal Irish Lancers, BI.  89. 6th Inniskilling Dragoons, W.M.  90. 10th Royal Hussars, BI.

**91.** 15th (King's) Hussars, BI. **92.** 14th (King's) Hussars. **93.** 19th Hussars. **94.** 18th (Queen Mary's Own) Hussars, 1911–22. **95.** 12th Lancers, BI. **96.** 17/21 Lancers (*cf*.18), post 1922 when 17th (Duke of Cambridge's Own) Lancers was united with 21st Lancers. **97.** 13th Hussars, 1901–22. **98.** 16th (The Queen's) Lancers, BI.

**99**. 21st (Empress of India) Lancers.  **100**. 20th Hussars.  **101**. 24th Lancers, W.M.
**102**. 27th Lancers, BI.  **103**. 23rd Hussars, BI.  **104**. 21st Lancers (points and butts of
lances missing).  **105**. 5th Royal Inniskilling Dragoon Guards.  **106**. Reconnaissance
Corps, disbanded 1946.

107. Royal Wiltshire Yeomanry, BI. 108. The Queen's Own Hussars. 109. 9th/12th Royal Lancers. 110. North Irish Horse. 111. Fife and Forfar Yeomanry, W.M. 112. Scottish Horse. 113. Welsh Horse. 114. 13/18th Royal Hussars. 115. 14th (King's) Hussars, BI, 1898–1915. 116. 15th/19th The King's Royal Hussars, post 1922. 117. South Irish Horse. 118. 14th/20th King's Hussars. Bronze. 119. 14th/20th King's Hussars with "FR" on chest. 120. Forage cap badge, 13th Hussars, post 1902.

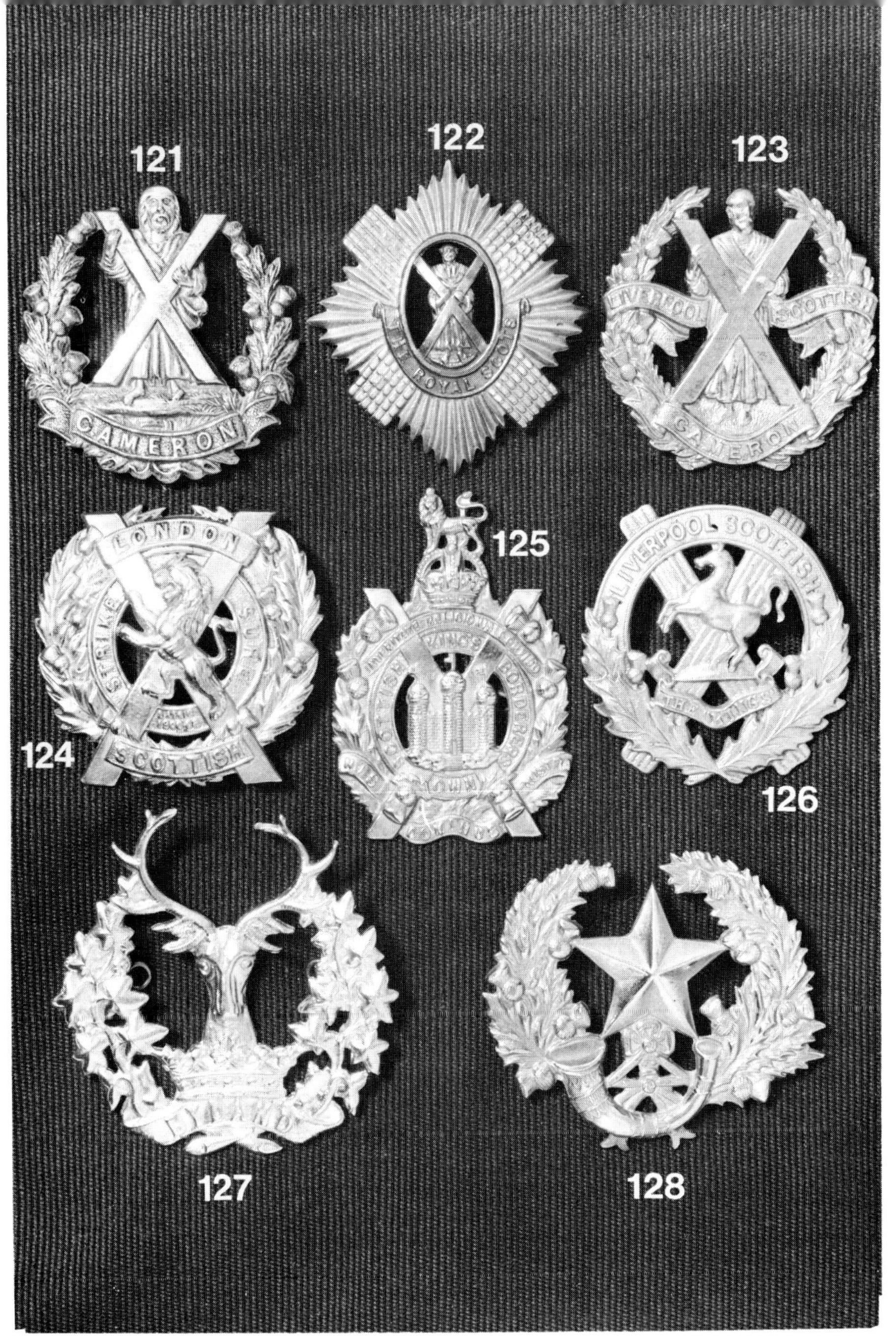

121. The Queen's Own Cameron Highlanders, W.M. 122. The Royal Scots, BI.
123. The Liverpool Scottish, W.M., 1937–69. 124. The London Scottish, W.M.
125. The King's Own Scottish Borderers, W.M. 126. 10th (Scottish) Battalion, The
King's (Liverpool) Regiment, W.M., 1908–37. 127. The Gordon Highlanders, W.M.
128. The Cameronians (Scottish Rifles), W.M.

**129.** Royal Scots Fusiliers. **130.** The Black Watch (Royal Highland Regiment). No title (*cf*.48), W.M. **131.** The Highland Light Infantry (City of Glasgow Regiment), W.M. **132.** Lovat Scouts, W.M. **133.** Argyll and Sutherland Highlanders, W.M. **134.** Lowland Regiment, W.M. **135.** The Glasgow Highlanders (The Highland Light Infantry), W.M. **136.** The Black Watch (*cf*.48 and 130), with title, W.M.

137. Lanarkshire Yeomanry, 1955–6.   138. Seaforth Highlanders, W.M.   139. Ayrshire (Earl of Carrick's Own) Yeomanry.   140. The Lowland Brigade, W.M.   141. Highland Brigade, anodised.   142. 5th Battn., Seaforth Highlanders, W.M., 1908–20.   143. Tyneside Scottish, W.M.

144. 8th (Irish) Battn. The King's Regiment (Liverpool).   145. Connaught Rangers.
146. Royal Munster Fusiliers, BI.   147. The Leinster Regiment, BI.   148. The Royal
Ulster Rifles, W.M.   149. Royal Dublin Fusiliers, BI.   150, 150a. Royal Irish Fusiliers,
BI.   151. Dublin Regiment, bronze.   152. The Royal Irish Regiment.

**153.** The Royal Fusiliers.  **154.** The Buffs (Royal East Kent Regiment).  **155.** Royal Northumberland Fusiliers, BI, 1935–60.  **156.** The King's Own Royal Regiment (Lancaster).  **157.** Northumberland Fusiliers, pre 1935.  **158.** The Queen's (Royal West Surrey Regiment), BI.  **159.** Royal Warwickshire Regiment, BI.

160. The Royal Lincolnshire Regiment, post 1946, BI. 161. The Lincolnshire Regiment, BI. 162. The Norfolk Regiment, BI, pre 1935. 163. The Devonshire Regiment. 164. Beret, The Royal Norfolk Regiment. 165. The Royal Norfolk Regiment, 1935–60. 166. The King's Regiment (Liverpool), BI, pre 1926. 167. The King's Regiment (Liverpool), BI, 1926–60.

168. The Suffolk Regiment, 1915–19.   169. The East Yorkshire Regiment, 1915–19.
170. West Yorkshire Regiment, BI.   171. The East Yorkshire Regiment, W.M., rose in centre.   172. West Yorkshire Regiment, BI.   173. The Suffolk Regiment (*cf.* 168), BI.
174. West Yorkshire Regiment.   175. 4th Battalion, The Somerset Light Infantry, W.M.   176. The Somerset Light Infantry, (Prince Albert's), W.M.

177. The Green Howards (Alexandra Princess of Wales' Own Yorkshire Regiment), bronze, 1908–1951. 178. The Green Howards (Alexandra Princess of Wales' Own Yorkshire Regiment), W.M., 1908–51. 179. The Green Howards (Alexandra Princess of Wales' Own Yorkshire Regiment), 1951–60. 180. The Green Howards (Alexandra Princess of Wales' Own Yorkshire Regiment), 1915–19. 181. The Bedfordshire Regiment, W.M., pre 1915. 182. The Leicestershire Regiment. 183. The Bedfordshire Regiment, BI, pre 1915. 184. The Hertfordshire Regiment. 185. The Royal Leicestershire Regiment (beret), post 1946. 186. The Bedfordshire Regiment, 1915–19. 187. The Bedfordshire and Hertfordshire Regiment, W.M., post 1919.

188. Royal Welsh Fusiliers, 1915–19.   189. The Lancashire Fusiliers, BI.   190. Royal Welch Fusiliers, BI, post 1920.   191. The South Wales Borderers, BI.   192. The Devonshire Regiment, topee badge.   193. The Cheshire Regiment, BI, post 1922. 194. The Cheshire Regiment, BI, 1898–1922.   195. The Royal Inniskilling Fusiliers, BI, post 1934.

**196.** The Worcestershire Regiment, pre 1925. **197.** The Worcestershire Regiment, BI, 1925–66. **198.** The East Lancashire Regiment, brass rose, W.M. **199.** The East Lancashire Regiment, rose, W.M. **200.** The East Lancashire Regiment, all brass, 1915–19. **201.** The Gloucestershire Regiment, small back badge. **202.** The Gloucestershire Regiment, W.M. **203.** The Gloucestershire Regiment, large back badge, BI.

204. The Duke of Wellington's Regiment (West Riding), BI.  205. The East Surrey Regiment, BI.  206. The Border Regiment, W.M., post 1953.  207. The Border Regiment, 1915–19.  208. The Duke of Cornwall's Light Infantry, W.M.  209. The East Surrey Regiment, 1915–19.  210. The East Surrey Regiment (with Imperial crown), BI.

**211.** The Dorsetshire Regiment, BI.  **212.** The South Staffordshire Regiment, BI. **213.** The Royal Hampshire Regiment, BI.  **214.** The Hampshire Regiment, pre 1946. **215.** The Royal Sussex Regiment, BI.  **216.** The Hampshire Regiment, Officer's pattern.  **217.** The Hampshire Regiment, officer's pattern, bronze.  **218.** 5th (Cinque Ports) Battn. Royal Sussex Regiment.

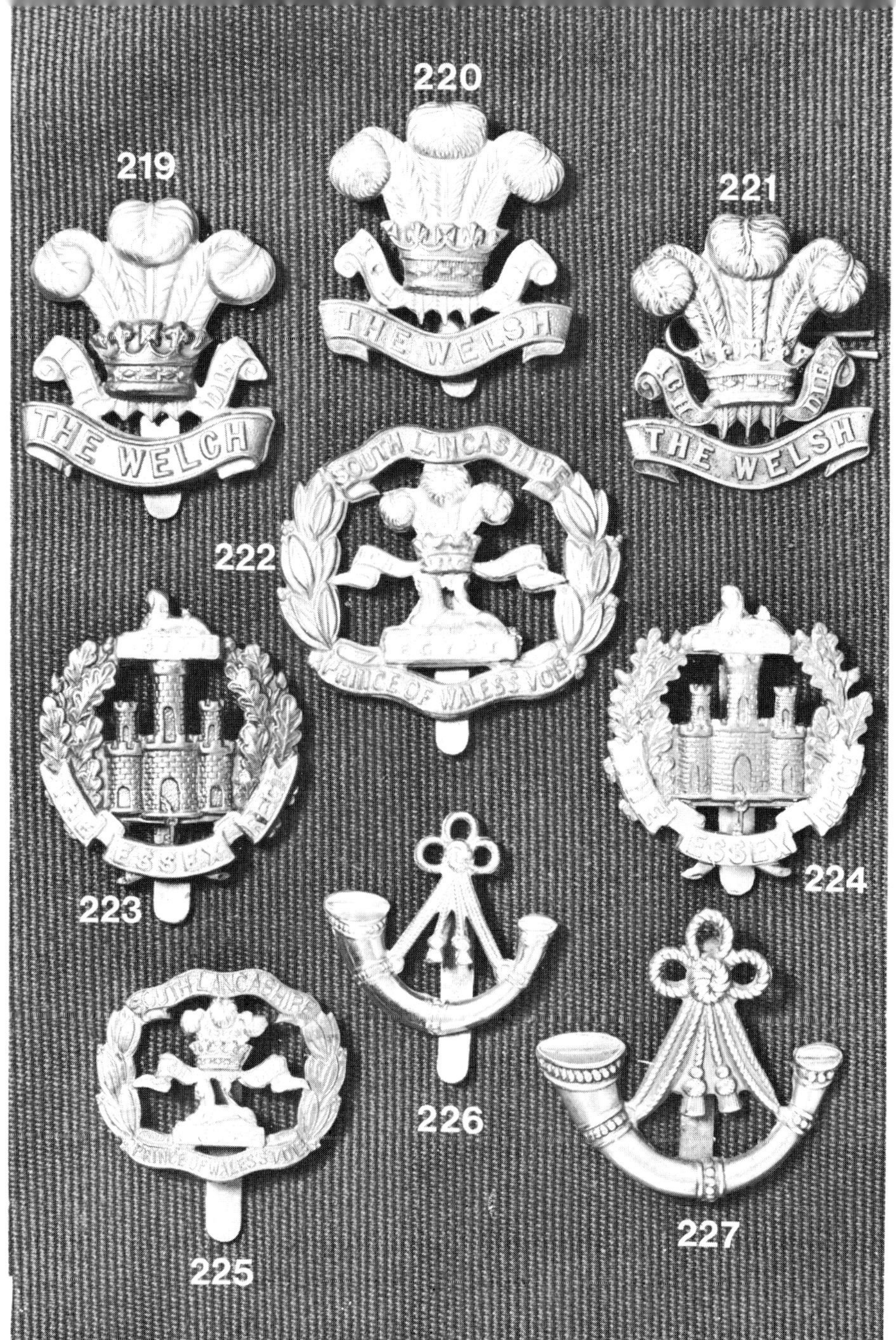

219. The Welch Regiment, BI.  220. The Welsh Regiment, BI, pre 1920.  221 The Welsh Regiment, W.M., pre 1920.  222. The South Lancashire (Prince of Wales' Volunteers), BI.  223. The Essex Regiment, BI.  224. The Essex Regiment (lacking Egypt on plinth), BI.  225. The South Lancashire (Prince of Wales' Volunteers), beret, BI.  226. The Oxfordshire and Buckinghamshire Light Infantry, beret, W.M. 227. The Oxfordshire and Buckinghamshire Light Infantry, W.M.

228. Royal Marine Artillery.   229. 7th (The Robin Hoods) Battn., Nottinghamshire and Derbyshire Regiment, W.M.   230. The Royal Berkshire Regiment.   231. The Sherwood Foresters (Nottinghamshire and Derbyshire Regiment), BI.   232. The Royal Marine Light Infantry.   233. The Royal Marines.   234. The Northamptonshire Regiment (with full key), W.M.   235. The Royal West Kent Regiment, W.M.   236. The Loyal North Lancashire Regiment, BI, 1902–20.

237. The Middlesex Regiment, BI.   238. The King's Shropshire Light Infantry, BI.
239. The Manchester Regiment, W.M.   240. The King's Own Yorkshire Light Infantry,
BI.   241. The King's Royal Rifle Corps.   242. The King's Shropshire Light Infantry,
beret, BI.   243. Officer's badge, The Middlesex Regiment, bronze.   244. The
Manchester Regiment, BI, pre 1923.   245. The Wiltshire Regiment.

246. The York and Lancaster Regiment, BI.  247. 6th Battalion, The Durham Light Infantry, beret, black. 248. The Durham Light Infantry, W.M. 249. The Rifle Brigade, W.M., 1911–34. 250. The Rifle Brigade (Prince Consort's Own), W.M., 1934–58. 251. The Loyal Regiment, BI, 1920–53. 252. The North Staffordshire Regiment, BI. 253. The North Staffordshire Regiment, 1915–19.

254. The Royal Air Force.  255. The Army Air Corps, W.M., 1942–50.  256. The Royal Flying Corps.  257. The Royal Artillery.  258. The Parachute Regiment, W.M. 259. The Honourable Artillery Company.  260. The Honourable Artillery Company, beret.  261. The Royal Artillery, beret.  262. Officer's badge, The Royal Artillery Territorial Force, bronze.  263. The 21st. S.A.S. Artists Rifles, W.M.  264. Dress Busby Badge, Royal Air Force, silver eagle, BI.

265. The Royal Army Service Corps, post 1953.   266. The Royal Army Service Corps, anodised, post 1953.   267. The Royal Army Medical Corps.   268. Royal Army Chaplains Department.   269. S.A.S. Regiment, anodised.   270. The Army Veterinary Corps, 1903–18.   271. The Army Service Corps, 1914–18.   272. Royal Army Service Corps, George VI.

**273.** Royal Army Dental Corps, BI.  **274.** Army Pay Corps, 1902–20.  **275.** Queen Alexandra's Royal Army Nursing Corps, 1949–54.  **276.** The Royal Corps of Signals, BI.  **277.** The Royal Army Pay Corps, 1920–29.  **278.** Royal Electrical and Mechanical Engineers, 1942–47.  **279.** Royal Corps of Signals, bronze.  **280.** Royal Electrical and Mechanical Engineers, BI, 1947–53.  **281.** Army Dental Corps, 1921–46.  **282.** Army Pay Corps.  **283.** Royal Army Pay Corps, W.M., 1929–53.

284. Army Educational Corps, 1920–46.   285. The Royal Pioneer Corps.   286. The Royal Army Educational Corps, bronze, post 1953.   287. Provost Staff.   288. The Royal Pioneer Corps, beret, bronze.   289. Royal Military Police, post 1953. 290. Corps of Military Police, George VI.

291. Royal Army Ordnance Corps, beret, BI, 1949–53.  292. Women's Legion, W.M.
293. Women's Royal Army Corps, BI, 1949–53.  294. Army Ordnance Corps, pre
1920.  295. Auxiliary Territorial Service.  296. Army Remount Service.  297. Royal
Army Ordnance Corps, 1920–47.  298. Royal Army Ordnance Corps with motto,
1947–49.

**299.** Honourable Artillery Company. **300.** Honourable Artillery Company, silver initials. **301.** Royal Horse Artillery, W.M. **302.** Army Physical Training Corps. **303.** Machine Gun Corps. **304.** Army Catering Corps, BI. **305.** Intelligence Corps. **306.** Junior Leaders Training Regiment.

307. Queen's Royal Surrey Regiment, anodised. 308. East Anglia Regiment, BI. 309. Queen's Regiment, anodised, post 1966. 310. Small Arms School Corps, W.M., post 1929. 311. Royal Military Academy Woolwich, BI. 312. Royal Military Academy Sandhurst, W.M. 313. National Defence Company. 314. Royal Military College, Sandhurst.

315. 3rd County of London Yeomanry (The Sharpshooters).   316. The City of London Yeomanry (Rough Riders), BI.  317. 3/4th County of London Yeomanry (Sharpshooters), BI.  318. Army Cyclist Corps.  319. Inns of Court O.T.C., bronze.  320. 1st King Edward's Horse (The King's Overseas Dominions Regiment).  321. Westminster Dragoons, W.M.  322. 2nd King Edward's Horse.  323. Inns of Court Regiment, pre 1961.

324. 5th City of London Regiment (London Rifle Brigade), W.M.   325. 10th London Regiment (Hackney), post 1912.   326. 5th City of London Regiment, with honours and scroll, (*cf.*324).   327. Royal Fusiliers (City of London Regiment).   328. 5th City of London Regiment Cadets (*cf.*324, 326).   329. 7th City of London Regiment. 330. 10th County of London Regiment (Paddington Rifles), 1908–12.   331. 11th London Regiment (Finsbury Rifles).   332. 8th Battn. City of London Regiment (Post Office Rifles).   333. 9th London Regiment (Queen Victoria's Rifles).

334. 18th London Regiment (London Irish Rifles). 335. Queen's Royal Rifles. 336. 19th London Regiment (St. Pancras). 337. 15th London Regiment (Prince of Wales' Own Civil Service Rifles). 338. 12th London Regiment (Rangers). 339. 23rd London Regiment (The East Surrey Regiment). 340. 16th County of London (Queen's Westminsters), pre 1921. 341. 16th London Regiment (Queen's Westminsters and Civil Service Rifles), post 1921. 342. 25th County of London (Cyclists). 343. 28th London Regiment (Artist's Rifles). 344. 13th London Regiment (Princess Louise's Kensington Regiment). 345. 24th London Regiment (The Queen's). 346. Officer, 20th London Regiment (The Queen's Own), BI.

347. The Queen's Own Yorkshire Yeomanry, 1956–69. 348. The Queen's Own Worcestershire Hussars. 349. The Warwickshire Yeomanry, W.M. 350. The Cambridgeshire Regiment, BI. 351. East Riding Yeomanry, BI. 352. Yorkshire Dragoons (Queen's Own), black. 353. Yorkshire Hussars (Alexandra, Princess of Wales' Own), BI.

354. The Lothian and Border Horse. 355. Duke of Lancaster's Own Yeomanry, bronze. 356. The Lothian and Border Horse, with tie and stalks. 357. Leicestershire Yeomanry (Prince Albert's Own), (*cf.*16). 358. North Somerset Yeomanry, W.M. 359. Shropshire Yeomanry. 360. Cheshire (Earl of Chester's) Yeomanry, BI. 361. Duke of Lancaster's Own Yeomanry.

362. 5th Battn. Border Regiment, W.M.  363. The Westmorland and Cumberland Yeomanry.  364. The Pembroke Yeomanry, BI.  365. The Royal East Kent Yeomanry. 366. The South Nottinghamshire Hussars.  367. The Northumberland Hussars, W.M. 368. The Northamptonshire Yeomanry, W.M.  369. The Hampshire Yeomanry (Carabiniers).

370. The West Somerset Yeomanry.  371. The Royal Devon Yeomanry Artillery.
372. The Royal Buckinghamshire Hussars.  373. The Queen's Own Dorset Yeomanry,
W.M., 1902–18.  374. The Queen's Own Dorset Yeomanry, post 1920.  375. The
Berkshire Yeomanry.  376. The Berkshire Imperial Yeomanry, W.M.

377. The Glamorgan Yeomanry, BI. 378. The Lancashire Hussars (Imperial Yeomanry). 379. The Essex Yeomanry. 380. The Sussex Yeomanry. 381. The Norfolk Yeomanry (The King's Own Royal Regiment). 382. The Surrey Yeomanry, W.M. 383. 1st Battn. Monmouthshire Regiment, W.M. 384. 2nd Battn. Monmouthshire Regiment. 385. Norfolk Yeomanry, beret.

386. The Lincolnshire Yeomanry.  387. The Leeds Rifles (Cockburn High School Cadets).  388. The Herefordshire Light Infantry, W.M.  389. 8th Battn. P.W.O. West Yorkshire Regiment (Leeds Rifles), black.  390. The Herefordshire Regiment, W.M. 391. The Loyal Suffolk Hussars.  392. 7/8th Battn. P.W.O. West Yorkshire Regiment (Leeds Rifles), black.  393. 6th Battn. Hampshire Regiment (Duke of Connaught's Own), W.M.

**394.** Middlesex Imperial Yeomanry, W.M.  **395.** Officer's badge, Yorkshire Brigade. (*cf.*353) Silver and gilt.  **396.** Tyneside Irish, 1914–19.  **397.** Huntingdonshire Home Guard.  **398.** The Buckinghamshire Battn. (Oxfordshire and Buckinghamshire Light Infantry).  **399.** The Mobile Defence Corps, BI.  **400.** Royal Observer Corps, W.M. **401.** The Princess of Wales' Own Yorkshire Regiment, BI, 1902–8.

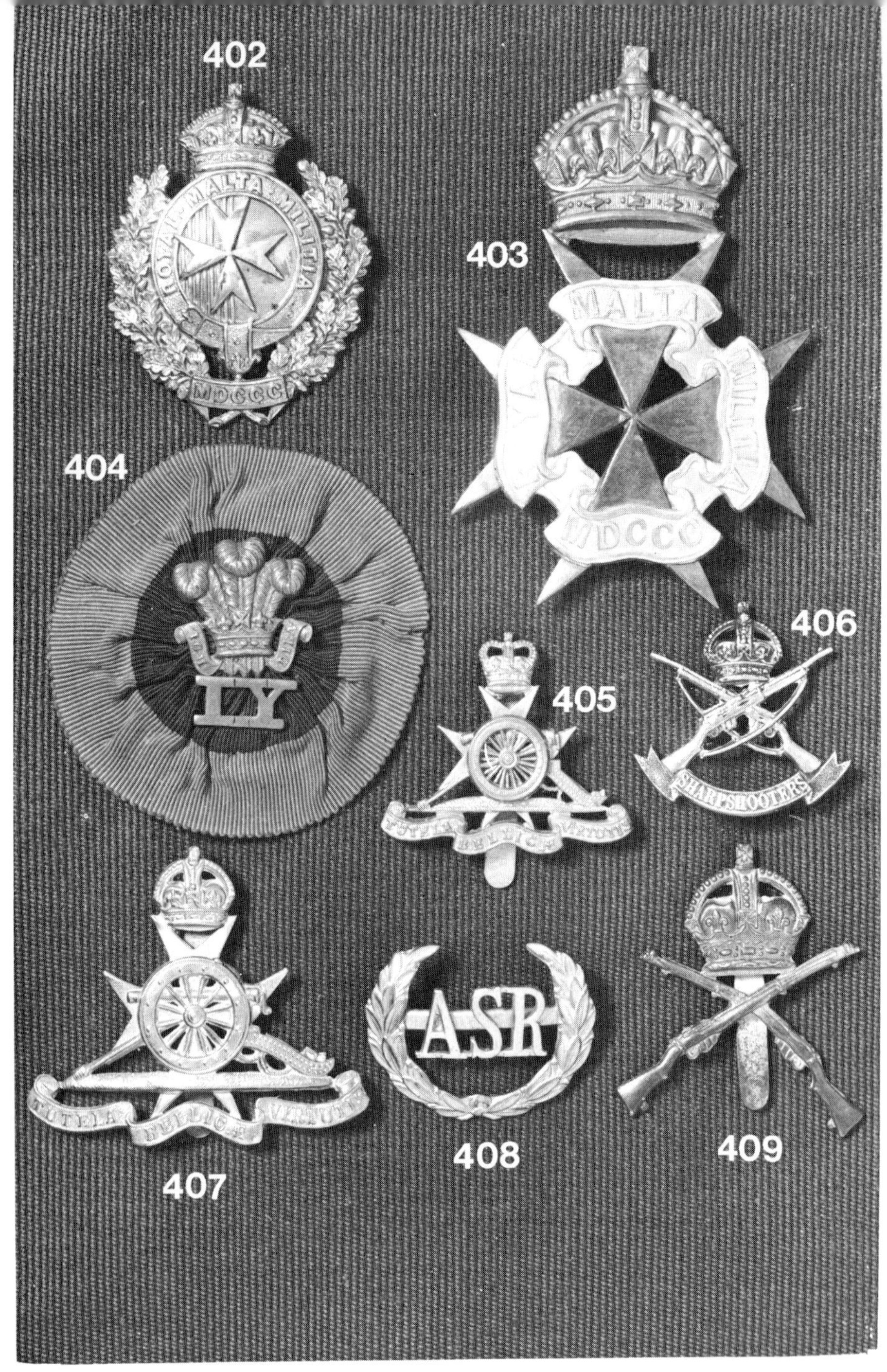

402. Royal Malta Militia, BI. 403. Royal Malta Militia shako, BI. 404. Imperial Yeomanry slouch hat with rosette. 405. Royal Malta Artillery beret. 406. Sharpshooters, BI (*cf.*315, 317). 407. Royal Malta Artillery, BI. 408. Army Scripture Readers, BI. 409. School of Musketry.

410. Royal Engineers, gilt.  411. National Defence Company.  412. Royal Engineers (George VI), BI.  413. Royal Engineers (Elizabeth II), BI.  414. Royal Engineers (George V, 1910–35), (*cf*.416).  415. Royal Engineers (Edward VII).  416. Royal Engineers (George V, 1915–19), (*cf*.414).

# BIBLIOGRAPHY

MUCH accurate information on badges worn by the British Army is to be found scattered through numerous magazines, regimental histories and order books. There are, however, a number of reliable volumes that will help identify most badges, and some of the more reasonably available titles are listed below.


*Army Badges and Insignia of World War II* by G. Rosignoli; London, 1972.

*Army Badges and Insignia Since 1945* by G. Rosignoli; London, 1973.

*Badges and Emblems of the British Forces 1940*; London, 1968.

*Battle Dress* by F. Wilkinson; London, 1970.

*Cavalry and Yeomanry Badges of the British Army, 1914* by F. Wilkinson; London, 1973.

*Collecting Military Antiques* by F. Wilkinson; London, 1977.

*Dress Regulations for the Army, 1900*, reprinted with an introduction by W. Y. Carman; London, 1969.

*Glengarry Badges of the British Line Regiments to 1881* by W. Y. Carman; London, 1973.

*Head-Dress Badges of the British Army* by A. Kipling and H. King; London, 1972.

*A History of the Uniforms of the British Army*, Vols. 1–5, by Cecil C. P. Lawson, London, 1961–66.

*Militaria* by F. Wilkinson; London, 1969.

*Military Badge Collecting* by J. Gaylor; London, 1971, 1977.

*Records and Badges of the British Army* by Major H. M. Chichester and Major G. Burgess-Short; Aldershot 1895 (2nd edition 1900), reprinted London, 1970.

*Regimental Badges* by Major T. J. Edwards; various editions, Aldershot, 1974.

*Regimental Badges in the British Army One Hundred Years Ago* by Edward Almack; London 1900, reprinted 1969.

*Scottish Regimental Badges 1793–1971* by W. H. and K. D. Bloomer; London, 1973.

*Shoulder Belt Plates and Buttons* by Major H. G. Parkyn; Aldershot, 1956.

A number of magazines contain occasional articles on badges:

*Battle*
*The Bulletin of the Military Historical Society*
*Dispatch* (Scottish Military Collectors)
*Journal of the Society for Army Historical Research*
*Soldier* (H.M.S.O.)
*Tradition*

# NOTES AND CORRECTIONS TO THE PLATE CAPTIONS

4 Silver and gilt

6 Helmet plate, Territorial Royal Artillery, 1902–22

7
9 } Although the centres are early examples, the main plates are modern Bandsmen's plates

12 Plate from officer's pouch of Army Medical Staff

16 Badge for pouch, not sabretache

17 Black

19 Wreath black, with cross of white metal

20 Black

21 Black

22 Shako plate, 1861–69

23 Glengarry badge, 1879–81

24 Officer's shako plate 1861–69, with silver centre

25 Black

26 Glengarry badge, post 1881

27 Officer's glengarry badge, 1881–98; gilt with silver centre

28 White metal

31 Officer's glengarry badge, post 1881

32 Silver and gilt

40 Puggaree badge

44 Volunteer badge

45 Black

46 Glengarry badge, black

47 Glengarry badge, black

49 Glengarry badge, bi-metal

52 George VI, bi-metal

64 White metal

68 Disbanded in 1922

71 Bi-metal

72 Disbanded in 1922; bi-metal

75 White metal

76 Bi-metal

77 Bi-metal

78 White metal

79 Bi-metal

82 Bi-metal

85 Bi-metal

88 Disbanded 1922

89 Bi-metal

91 Disbanded 1922

92 Disbanded 1922

93 White metal

94 White metal

97 Bi-metal

98 Disbanded 1922

101 Disbanded 1922

102 Disbanded 1922

103 Disbanded 1922

104 Bi-metal

105 White metal

108 Bi-metal

109 Anodised

112 Officer's badge

113 Bronze

115 Bi-metal

116 Bi-metal

134 Disbanded 1949

144 White metal

146 Disbanded 1922

147 Disbanded 1922

149 Disbanded 1922

151 Dublin National Volunteers

157 Disbanded 1922

163 Bi-metal

174 Bronze collar badge

179 White metal

182 Bi-metal

199 Militia badge

224 Volunteer badge

241 Black

268 Black

287 Norfolk Yeomanry

299 Militia Badge

300 Warrant officer's cap badge

308 Officer's badge in silver and gilt

320 Delete '1st'

| 326 | White metal | 350 | Note absence of 'E' in spelling of title |
| 327 | 1898–1901 | | |
| 329 | Bi-metal | 355 | Bronze |
| 330 | Black | 390 | Bi-metal |
| 347 | White metal | 391 | Bi-metal |
| 349 | County badge, and certainly worn at one time by Girl Guides | 398 | Black |

# INDEX

Air Force, Royal — 254, 264
Alexandra, Princess of Wales' Own Yorkshire Regiment — 177, 178, 179, 180, 401
Alexandra, Princess of Wales' Own Hussars — 353
Anglia Regiment, East — 308
Argyll and Sutherland Highlanders — 133
Armoured Corps, Royal — 61, 62
Army Air Corps — 255
    Catering Corps — 304
    Chaplains Department, Royal — 268
    Cyclist Corps — 318
    Dental Corps — 281
    Education Corps — 284
    Ordnance Corps — 294, 297, 298
    Pay Corps — 274, 282
    Physical Training Corps — 302
    Remount Service — 296
    Scripture Readers — 408
    Service Corps — 271
    Veterinary Corps — 270
Artillery, Royal Regiment of — 6, 38, 257, 261
    Devon Yeomanry — 371
    Horse — 301
    Malta — 405, 407
    Marine — 228
    Territorial Force — 6, 262
Artists' Rifles — 263, 343
Auxiliary Territorial Service — 295
Ayrshire (Earl of Carrick's Own) Yeomanry — 139

Bays, Queen's (2nd Dragoon Guards) — 69
Bedfordshire and Hertfordshire Regiment — 187
Bedfordshire Regiment — 181, 183, 186
Berkshire Regiment, Royal — 230
Berkshire Yeomanry — 375, 376
Black Watch (Royal Highlanders) — 48, 130, 136
Border Horse, Lothian and — 354, 356
Border Regiment — 14, 206, 207
    5th Battalion — 362
Borderers, King's Own Scottish — 125
Borderers, South Wales — 191
Buckinghamshire Battalion, Oxfordshire and Light Infantry — 398
Buckinghamshire Hussars, Royal — 372
Buckinghamshire, Oxfordshire and Light Infantry — 226, 227
Buffs (Royal East Kent Regiment) — 154

Cadets, 5th City of London Regiment — 328
Cadets, Cockburn High School — 387
Cambridge Regiment — 350
Cameron Highlanders, Queen's Own — 121
Cameronians (Scottish Rifles) — 128
Carabiniers, 3rd Dragoon Guards — 72, 79
Carabiniers, 6th Dragoon Guards — 26, 77
Carabiniers, Hampshire Yeomanry — 369
Catering Corps, Army — 304
Chaplains Department, Royal Army — 268
Cheshire Regiment — 193, 194
Cheshire (Earl of Chester's) Yeomanry — 360
Cinque Ports (5th Battalion Royal Sussex Regiment) — 218
City of London Regiment Cadets, 5th — 328
Civil Service Rifles — 337, 341

Cockburn High School Cadets, (The Leeds Rifles) — 387
Coldstream Guards — 56
College, Royal Military (Sandhurst) — 12
Connaught Rangers — 145
Corps, Army Air — 255
    Catering — 304
    Cyclists — 318
    Dental — 283
    Education — 286
    Ordnance — 294, 197, 298
    Pay — 274, 282
    Physical Training — 302
    Service, and Royal — 271
    Veterinary — 270
    Intelligence — 305
    King's Royal Rifle — 17, 25, 241
    Machine Gun — 303
    Mobile Defence — 399
    of Military Police — 290
    Queen Alexandra's Royal Army Nursing — 275
    Reconnaissance — 106
    Small Arms School — 310
    Tank — 63, 65, 66
County Down Regiment, Royal — 5
Cumberland Regiment — 14
Cumberland, Westmorland and Yeomanry — 363
Cyclist Corps, Army — 318
Cyclist, 25th County of London — 342

Defence Corps, Mobile — 399
Defence Corps, National — 411
Defence Company, National — 313
Dental Corps, Royal — 273
Derbyshire Regiment, Nottinghamshire and — 229, 231
Derbyshire Regiment (Sherwood Foresters) — 22, 50
Devonshire Regiment — 163, 192
Devonshire Yeomanry Artillery, Royal — 371
Dorsetshire Regiment — 211
Dorsetshire Yeomanry, Queen's Own — 373, 374
Dragoons, 1st Royal — 74, 76, 82
    2nd (Royal Scots Greys) — 80
    6th Inniskilling — 89
    Westminster — 321
    Yorkshire — 352
Dragoon Guards, 1st King's — 67, 70, 73, 74
    2nd (Queen's Bays) — 69
    3rd (Prince of Wales') — 72, 79
    4th Royal Irish — 68
    4th/7th Royal — 75
    5th — 71
    5th Royal Inniskilling — 105
    6th (Carabiniers) — 20, 77
    7th — 78
Dublin County Light Infantry — 26
Dublin Fusiliers, Royal — 149
Dublin National Volunteers — 151
Duke of Cambridge's Own (17th Lancers) — 18
    Connaught's Own, 6th Battalion Hampshire Regiment — 393
    Cornwall's Light Infantry — 208
    Lancaster's Own Yeomanry — 355, 361
    Wellington's Regiment (West Riding) — 204
Durham Light Infantry — 247, 248

Earl of Carrick's Own (Ayrshire Yeomanry)   139
Earl of Chester's Own (Cheshire Yeomanry)   360
East Anglia Regiment   308
    Kent Regiment, Royal (Buffs)   154
    Kent Yeomanry, Royal   365
    Lancashire Regiment   198, 199, 200
    Norfolk Regiment   2
    Riding Yeomanry   351
    Surrey Regiment   205, 209, 210, 339
    Surrey Regiment, 3rd Volunteer
       Battalion   47
    Yorkshire Regiment   169, 171
Education Corps, Army   284, 286
Electrical and Mechanical Engineers, Royal   278, 280
Empress of India's 21st Lancers   99
Engineer Volunteers   13
Engineers, Royal   410, 412 – 416
Essex Regiment   223
    Volunteers   224
    Yeomanry   379

Fife and Forfar Yeomanry   111
Finsbury Rifles   331
Foot, 9th Regiment of   2
    17th Regiment of   3
    34th Regiment of   14
    80th Regiment of   1
    86th Regiment of   5
    93rd Regiment of   23
    95th Regiment of   22
Fusiliers, Lancashire   44, 189
    Royal   153, 327
       Dublin   149
       Inniskilling   31, 195
       Irish   150, 150a
       Munster   146
       Northumberland   155, 157
       Scots   129
       Welch   188
       Welsh   190

General Officers   36
Glamorgan Yeomanry   377
Glasgow Highlanders (Highland Light Infantry)   135
Glasgow Regiment, City of (Highland Light
    Infantry)   131
Gloucestershire Regiment   201, 202, 203
Gordon Highlanders   39, 41, 127
Green Howards   177, 178, 179, 180, 401
Grenadier Guards   51, 52
Greys, Royal Scots (2nd Dragoons)   80
Guards, Coldstream   56
    Grenadier   51, 52
    Irish   58
    Life   53, 59, 60
    Royal Horse   55
    Scots   29, 30, 32
    Welsh   57

Hackney, 10th London Regiment   325
Hampshire Regiment   214, 216, 217
    Royal   213
    6th Battalion   393
    Yeomanry, Carabiniers   369
Herefordshire Light Infantry   388
Herefordshire Regiment   390
Hertfordshire Regiment   184
Hertfordshire Regiment, Bedfordshire and   187
Highland Brigade   141
    Light Infantry   37, 131, 135
    Regiment, Royal (Black Watch)   48, 130, 136

Highlanders, Argyll and Sutherland   133
    Glasgow (H.L.I.)   135
    Gordon   39, 41, 127
    Queen's Own Cameron   121
    Seaforth   138
    5th Battalion, Seaforth   142
    Sutherland   23
Honourable Artillery Company   259, 260, 299, 300
Home Guard, Huntingdonshire   397
Horse Artillery, Royal   301
    Guards, Royal   55
    King Edward's   320, 322
    Lothian and Border   354, 356
    North Irish   110
    Scottish   112
    South Irish   117
    Welsh   113
Household Cavalry   54
Huntingdonshire Home Guard   397
Hussars, 3rd, The King's Own   81
    4th, Queen's Own   21, 84
    7th, Queen's Own   83
    8th, King's Own Irish   85
    10th Royal   90
    11th, Prince Albert's Own   87
    13th   49, 97, 120
    13th/18th Royal   114
    14th King's   92, 115
    14th/20th King's   118, 119
    15th King's   91
    15th/19th King's Royal   116
    18th, and Queen Mary's Own   45, 94
    19th   93
    20th   100
    23rd   103
    Lancashire (Imperial Yeomanry)   378
    Loyal Suffolk   391
    Northumberland   367
    Queen's Own   108
    Queen's Own Oxfordshire   42
    Queen's Own Worcestershire   348
    Royal Buckinghamshire   372
    South Nottinghamshire   366
    Yorkshire   353

Imperial Yeomanry   404
    Berkshire   376
    Lancashire Hussars   378
    Middlesex   394
Inniskilling Dragoon Guards, 5th Royal   71, 105
    Dragoons, 6th   89
    Fusiliers, Royal   31, 195
Inns of Court O.T.C.   319
    Regiment   323
Intelligence Corps   305
Irish Dragoon Guards, 4th Royal   68
    Fusiliers, Royal   150, 150a
    Guards   58
    Horse, North   110
       South   117
    Hussars, 8th King's Own   85
    Lancers, 5th Royal   88
    Rifles, London   334
       Royal   5, 43
       Tyneside   396

Junior Leaders Training Regiment   306

Kensington Regiment, Princess Louise's   344
Kent Regiment, Royal East (Buffs)   154
    Royal West   235
    Yeomanry, Royal East   365

King Edward's Horse 320, 322
King's Dragoon Guards, 1st 67, 70, 73, 74
   Hussars, 14th 92, 115
     14th/20th 118, 119
     15th 91
   Overseas Dominions Regiment 320
   Regiment (Liverpool) 166, 167
     8th Irish Battalion 144
     10th Scottish Battalion 126
   Royal Hussars, 15th/19th 116
     Rifle Corps 17, 25, 241
   Shropshire Light Infantry 238, 242
   Own 2nd Staffordshire Militia 4
     Hussars, 3rd 81
     Irish Hussars, 8th 85
     Royal Regiment (Lancaster) 156
     Royal Regiment (Norfolk Yeomanry) 381, 385
     Scottish Borderers 125
     Yorkshire Light Infantry 40, 240

Lanarkshire Yeomanry 137
Lancashire Fusiliers 44, 189
   Regiment, East 198, 199, 200
     North (Loyal) 236, 251
     South (Prince of Wales' Vol's) 222, 225
Lancaster (King's Own Royal Regiment) 156
Lancaster's Duke of Yeomanry 355, 361
Lancers, 5th Royal Irish 88
   9th Queen's Royal 86
   9th/12th Royal 109
   12th 95
   16th (The Queen's) 98
   17th (Duke of Cambridge's Own) 18
   17th/21st 96
   21st (Empress of India) 99, 104
   24th 101
   27th 102
Leeds Rifles 387, 389, 392
Legion, Women's 292
Leicestershire Regiment and Royal 3, 182, 185
   Yeomanry 16, 357
Leinster Regiment 147
Life Guards 53, 59, 60
Light Infantry, Dublin County 26
   Duke of Cornwall's 208
   Durham 247, 248
   Herefordshire 388
   Highland 37, 131, 135
Light Infantry, King's Own Yorkshire 40, 240
   King's Shropshire 238, 242
   Oxfordshire and Buckinghamshire 226, 227
   Oxfordshire and Buckinghamshire,
     Buckinghamshire Battalion 398
   Royal Marine 232
   Somerset (Prince Albert's) 176
   Somerset, 4th Battalion 175
Lincolnshire, Regiment 161
   Royal Regiment 160
   Yeomanry 386
Liverpool Regiment (King's) 166, 167
   8th (Irish) Battalion 144
   10th (Scottish) Battalion 126
   Scottish 123
London, 5th City of, Regiment (London
   Rifle Brigade) 324, 326
   5th City of, Regiment (London Rifle
     Brigade) Cadets 328
   7th City of, 329
   8th Battalion City of, (Post Office Rifles) 332
   9th (Queen Victoria's Rifles) 333
   10th County of, (Paddington Rifles) 330

10th (Hackney) 325
11th (Finsbury Rifles) 331
12th (Rangers) 338
13th (Princess Louise's Kensington
   Regiment) 344
15th (Prince of Wales' Own Civil Service
   Rifles) 337
16th County of, Regiment (Queen's
   Westminsters) 340, 341
17th Regiment (Tower Hamlets) 11
18th Regiment (London Irish Rifles) 334
19th Regiment (St. Pancras) 336
20th Regiment (Queen's Own) 346
23rd Regiment (East Surrey) 339
24th Regiment (Queen's) 345
25th County of, Regiment (Cyclists) 342
28th Regiment (Artist's Rifles) 343
Scottish 124
Yeomanry, City of, (Rough Riders) 316
Yeomanry, County of, (Sharpshooters) 315, 317
Lothian and Border Horse 354, 356
Lovat Scouts 132
Lowland Brigade 140
Lowland Regiment 134
Loyal Regiment (North Lancashire) 236, 251
Loyal Suffolk Hussars 391

Machine Gun Corps 303
Malta Artillery, Royal 405, 407
Malta Militia 402, 403
Manchester Regiment 239, 244
Marine Artillery, Royal 228
Marine Light Infantry, Royal 232
Marines, Royal 233
Medical Corps, Royal Army 267
Middlesex Imperial Yeomanry 394
Middlesex Regiment 10, 237, 243
Military Academy, Royal (Sandhurst) 312
   Academy, Royal (Woolwich) 311
   College, Royal (Sandhurst) 12, 314
   Police, Corps of 290
     Royal 289
Militia, King's Own 2nd Staffordshire 4
Militia, Royal Malta 402, 403
Mobile Defence Corps 399
Monmouthshire Regiment, 1st Battalion 383
Monmouthshire Regiment, 2nd Battalion 384
Munster Fusiliers, Royal 146

National Defence Company 313, 411
Nottinghamshire and Derbyshire Regiment
   (Sherwood Foresters) 231
   7th Battalion (Robin Hoods) 229
   Hussars, South 366
Norfolk Regiment, and Royal 33, 162, 164, 165
   East 2
   Yeomanry (King's Own Royal Regiment) 381, 385
North Irish Horse 110
   Lancashire (Loyal Regiment) 236, 251
   Somerset Yeomanry 358
   Staffordshire Regiment 9, 252, 253
Northamptonshire Regiment 234
Northamptonshire Yeomanry 368
Northumberland Fusiliers, and Royal 155, 157
Northumberland Hussars 367
Nursing Corps, Queen Alexandra's Royal
   Army 257

Observer Corps, Royal 400
Ordnance Corps, Army 294
   Royal 291, 297, 298

Overseas Dominions Regiment, King's 320
Oxfordshire and Buckinghamshire Light
   Infantry 226, 227
Oxfordshire and Buckinghamshire,
   Buckinghamshire Battalion 398
Oxfordshire Hussars, Queen's Own 42

Paddington Rifles 330
Parachute Regiment 258
Pay Corps, Army 274, 282
   Royal 277, 283
Pembroke Yeomanry 364
Physical Training Corps, Army 302
Pioneer Corps, Royal 285, 288
Police, Corps of Military 290
   Royal 289
Post Office Rifles 332
Prince Albert's Own 11th Hussars 87
   Own Leicestershire Yeomanry 16, 357
   Somerset Light Infantry 176
     4th Battalion 175
Prince Consort's Own, (Rifle Brigade) 250
Prince of Wales' Dragoon Guards, 3rd 72, 79
   Own Civil Service Rifles 337, 341
   Own West Yorkshire Regiment. Leeds
     Rifles 389, 392
   Volunteers, South Lancashire Regiment 222, 225
Princess Louise's Kensington Regiment 344
Princess of Wales' Own Yorkshire Hussars 353
Princess of Wales' Own Yorkshire
   Regiment 177, 178, 179, 180, 401

Queen Alexandra's Royal Army Nursing Corps 275
Queen Mary's Own 18th Hussars 45, 94
Queen Victoria's Rifles 333
Queen's Bays (2nd D.G.'s) 69
   Lancers, 16th 98
   Own 20th London Regiment 346
     Cameron Highlanders 121
     Dorset Yeomanry 373, 374
     Hussars 108
     Hussars, 4th 21, 84
     Hussars, 7th 83
     Oxfordshire Hussars 42
     Worcestershire Hussars 348
     Yorkshire Dragoons, 352
     Yorkshire Yeomanry 347
   Regiment 309, 345
   Royal Lancers, 9th 86
     Rifles 335
     Surrey Regiment 307
     West Surrey Regiment 8, 24, 158
   Westminsters, 16th County of London
     Regiment 340

Rangers, (12th London Regiment) 338
Rangers, Connaught 145
Reconnaissance Corps 106
Remount Service, Army 296
Rifle Brigade 249, 250
   Brigade, 5th City of London Regiment 324, 326
   Brigade, 5th City of London Regiment,
     Cadets 328
   Corps, King's Royal 17, 25, 241
   Regiment, West Meath 19
   Volunteer Corps, 4th Surrey 46
Rifles, Artist's 263, 343
   Civil Service 337, 341
   Finsbury 331
   Leeds 387, 389, 392
   London Irish 334
   Paddington 330

Post Office 332
Queen's Royal 335
Queen Victoria's 333
Royal Irish 5, 43
Royal Ulster 148
Scottish (Cameronians) 128
Robin Hoods 229
Royal Armoured Corps 61, 62
   Army Chaplains' Department 268
     Dental Corps 273
     Educational Corps 286
     Medical Corps 267
     Ordnance Corps 291
     Pay Corps 277, 283
     Service Corps 265, 266, 272
   Artillery 6, 38, 257, 261, 262
   Artillery Territorial Force 6, 262
   Buckinghamshire Hussars 372
   Corps of Signals 276, 279
   Devon Artillery 371
   East Kent Regiment 154
   Flying Corps 256
   Fusiliers 153
   Horse Artillery 301
   Malta Artillery 405, 407
   Observer Corps 400
   Pioneer Corps 285, 288
   Regiment (Royal Scots) 122
   Scots Greys 80

S.A.S. 269
S.A.S., 21st Artists' Rifles 263
Sabretache, Victorian Cypher 15
St. Pancras, 19th London Regiment 336
Sandhurst, Royal Military College 12, 312, 314
School of Musketry 409
Scots Fusiliers, Royal 129
   Greys, Royal (2nd Dragoons) 80
   Guards 29, 30, 32
   , Royal (The Royal Regiment) 122
Scottish, 10th Battalion, King's Liverpool
   Regiment, 126
   Borderers, King's Own 125
   Liverpool 123, 126
   London 124
   Horse 112
   Rifles (Cameronians) 128
   Tyneside 143
Seaforth Highlanders 138
Seaforth Highlanders, 5th Battalion 142
Service Corps, Army 271
   Royal 265, 266
Sharpshooters, (County of London
   Yeomanry) 315, 317
Sherwood Foresters 22, 50, 231
Shropshire Light Infantry, King's 238, 242
Shropshire Yeomanry 359
Signals, Royal Corps of 276, 279
Small Arms School Corps 310
Somerset Light Infantry (Prince Albert's) 176
   Light Infantry (Prince Albert's) 4th
     Battalion 175
   Yeomanry, North 358
   Yeomanry, West 370
South Irish Horse 117
   Lancashire Regiment (Prince of Wales'
     Volunteers) 222, 225
   Nottinghamshire Hussars 366
   Staffordshire Regiment 1, 28, 212
   Wales Borderers 191
Staffordshire Militia, King's Own 2nd 4

Staffordshire Regiment North                          252, 253
Staffordshire Regiment South                          1, 28, 212
Suffolk Hussars, Loyal                                391
Suffolk Regiment                                      168, 173
Surrey Regiment East                   47, 205, 209, 210, 339
    Regiment West, Royal                              8, 24, 158
    Regiment Queen's Royal                            307
    Rifle Volunteer Corps, 4th                        46
    Yeomanry                                          382
Sussex Regiment Royal                                 215, 218
Sussex Yeomanry                                       380
Sutherland Highlanders                                23

Tank Corps                                            63, 65, 66
Tank Regiment, Royal                                  64
Territorial Force, Royal Artillery                    262
Territorial Service, Auxiliary                        295
Tower Hamlets Regiment (17th London)                  11
Training Regiment Junior Leaders                      306
Tyneside Irish                                        396
Tyneside Scottish                                     143

Ulster Rifles, Royal                                  148

Veterinary Corps, Army                                270
Victorian Cypher, Sabretache                          15
Volunteer's, Engineer                                 13

Warwickshire Regiment, Royal                 7, 34, 35, 159
Warwickshire, Yeomanry                                349
Welch Fusiliers, Royal                                190
Welch Regiment                                        219
Welsh Fusiliers, Royal                                188
Welsch Guards                                         57
Welsh Horse                                           113
Welsh Regiment                                        220, 221
West Kent, Royal Regiment                             235
    Meath Rifle Regiment                              19
    Riding Regiment (Duke of Wellington's)            204
    Somerset Yeomanry                                 370
    Surrey Regiment, Royal                            8, 24, 158
    Yorkshire Regiment                       170, 172, 174
    Yorkshire Regiment, (Prince of Wales'
        Leeds Rifles)                                 389, 392
Westminster Dragoons                                  321
Westmorland and Cumberland Yeomanry                   363
Wiltshire Yeomanry, Royal                             107
Wiltshire Regiment                                    245
Women's Legion                                        292

Women's Royal Army Corps                              293
Woolwich, Royal Military Academy                      311
Worcestershire Hussars, Queen's Own                   348
Worcestershire Regiment                               196, 197

Yeomanry, Ayrshire (Earl of Carrick's Own)            139
    Berkshire                                         375, 176
    Cheshire (Earl of Chester's Own)                  360
    City of London (Rough Riders)                     316
    County of London (Sharpshooters)                  315, 317
    Duke of Lancaster's Own                           355, 361
    East Riding                                       351
    Essex                                             379
    Fife and Forfar                                   111
    Glamorgan                                         377
    Hampshire (Carabiniers)                           369
    Imperial                            376, 378, 394, 404
    Lanarkshire                                       137
    Leicestershire (Prince Albert's Own)             16, 357
    Lincolnshire                                      386
    Middlesex Imperial                                394
    Norfolk                                           381, 385
    North Somerset                                    358
    Northamptonshire                                  368
    Pembroke                                          364
    Queen's Own Dorset                                373, 374
    Queen's Own Yorkshire                             347
    Royal Devon, Artillery                            371
    Royal East Kent                                   365
    Royal Wiltshire                                   107
    Shropshire                                        359
    Surrey                                            382
    Sussex                                            380
    Warwickshire                                      349
    West Somerset                                     370
    Westmorland and Cumberland                        363
York and Lancaster Regiment                           246
Yorkshire Brigade                                     395
    Dragoons                                          352
    Hussars                                           353
    Light Infantry, King's Own                        40, 240
    Regiment (Alexandra, Princess of Wales'
        Own Green Howards)   177, 178, 179, 180, 401
        East                                      169, 171
        West                                  170, 172, 174
        West (Prince of Wales' Own Leeds
            Rifles) 7th/8th Battalion                 392
        West (Prince of Wales' Own) 8th
            Battalion                                 389